Summary
of

The Storied Life of A. J. Fikry
Gabrielle Zevin

Conversation Starters

By BookHabits

Tips for Using BookHabits Conversation Starters:

EVERY GOOD BOOK CONTAINS A WORLD FAR DEEPER THAN the surface of its pages. The characters and their world come alive through the words on the pages, yet the characters and its world still live on. Questions herein are designed to bring us beneath the surface of the page and invite us into the world that lives on. These questions can be used to:

- Foster a deeper understanding of the book
- Promote an atmosphere of discussion for groups
- Assist in the study of the book, either individually or corporately
- Explore unseen realms of the book as never seen before

About Us:

THROUGH YEARS OF EXPERIENCE AND FIELD EXPERTISE, from newspaper featured book clubs to local library chapters, *BookHabits* can bring your book discussion to life. Host your book party as we discuss some of today's most widely read books.

Table of Contents

Introducing *The Storied Life of A. J. Fikry*

*T*HE STORIED LIFE OF AJ FIKRY IS ABOUT AJ, A LONELY MAN living on a small island. He owns a bookshop but is rude, grumpy, and doesn't mix with anyone. He has eclectic tastes, and when a new female sales representative is assigned to him, they don't get along at first. Then, a child is abandoned in his bookshop, and his life changes. Amelia, who first comes to sell books to AJ, soon finds herself in a deep emotional connection with him and Maya, the abandoned child. The story unfolds gradually and soon includes all the inhabitants of the island.

The stories of the others living on the island are also explored in the book, including a philandering husband, a failed writer who sleeps with everything that moves, and his long-suffering wife, Ismay. Also, a police officer who goes from being a shy and reserved man to someone who becomes the mainstay of the community through his efforts.

The island-dwellers lead lives that often overlap the lives of others, and everyone is closely connected to each other. Nic, Ismay's sister, was AJ's wife, and upon her death, Ismay keeps an eye out for AJ but doesn't hesitate to steal from him either. Daniel is the abandoned child's real father but doesn't take responsibility for the child. It is AJ who adopts Maya when her mother, Marian, commits suicide. Thus, everyone is connected with the strong threads of fate.

There is an underlying sub-plot of financial constraints. Marian takes her own life because she can see a life of penury ahead for her and her daughter. AJ doesn't work to improve his bookshop, so his profits have reduced. He has a copy of *Tamerlane*, which he keeps as retirement insurance, but Ismay steals this manuscript and gives it to Marian so she can have money to take care of Maya. In the end, the money from the manuscript causes Amelia to argue with both Maya and AJ, the latter of which shows AJ's selfless side for the first time.

The book tightly binds all these elements on a background of books and literature, making an emotional read for book lovers.

Introducing the Author

GABRIELLE ZEVIN IS AN AMERICAN AUTHOR WHO HAS written eight books in her career spanning nine years, including *The Storied Life of AJ Fikry*, her latest book, which was published in 2014. All of her books have been very well received. She won several awards for her first book, *Elsewhere*, including the Borders Original Voices Award. It was also nominated for the Quills Award and was included on the Carnegie longlist. Zevinfirst five books were in the young adult genre. Today, she is well established as a writer of contemporary fiction and young adult books. Her books have been translated into more than twenty languages.

Zevin grew up in Manhattan in New York and has recently moved to Los Angeles. Born to a Korean mother and a Jewish father, she claims that she has often felt different than others. Her academic background includes a degree in English and American Literature from Harvard University. She held her first writing job as a music critic for a local newspaper when she was a teenager.

Zevin is also an accomplished screenwriter. She wrote the screenplay for *Conversations with Other Women*, a movie released in 2005 starring Helena Bonham Carter and Aaron Eckhart. It was well received and has an IMDB rating of seven. She received an Independent Spirit Award for her work on the movie. Zevin has also contributed in adapting her novel to a Japanese film called *Darekaga Watashini Kiss woShita*. Apart from this, Zevin has also tried her hand at writing for the *New York Times Book Review* and *All Things Considered*, a news program on the radio.

A versatile and talented writer, Gabrielle Zevin has a quirky and fun style that resonates with most readers.

Discussion Questions

"Get Ready to Enter a New World"

Tip: Begin with questions dealing with broader issues to ensure ample time for quality discussions. Read through all discussion questions before engaging.

~ ~ ~

question 1

AJ used to be rather grumpy before Maya came into his life. How exactly did his outlook on life change after he adopted the little girl?

~ ~ ~

~ ~ ~

question 2

AJ adopted Maya and later married Amelia. What do you think about their small family? Do you consider them a functional family? Why or why not?

~ ~ ~

~ ~ ~

question 3

Daniel was a one-book wonder. He was married to Ismay and the biological father of Maya. What do you think of Daniel as an author and a character?

~ ~ ~

~ ~ ~

question 4

Daniel died in a car crash. Do you think Daniel committed suicide or was it an accident? Give evidence from the book to support your answer.

~ ~ ~

~ ~ ~

question 5

Lambiase was the police officer in charge of the island. He is a sympathetic character, but we gradually see him develop an interest in books. How do you see Lambiase's character development throughout the story? In what way is his gradual growth as a person interesting?

~ ~ ~

~ ~ ~

question 6

Marian Wallace is Maya's mother, and she abandons Maya because of lack of money. What do you think of her character and the decisions she took regarding her child?

~ ~ ~

~ ~ ~

question 7

Lambiase discovered that Ismay had stolen AJ's copy of *Tamerlane,* but he did not ask Ismay about it even though he was the officer in charge of finding the manuscript. Did your opinion of Lambiase change after discovering that he refrained from mentioning the theft? Why or why not?

~ ~ ~

~ ~ ~

question 8

Literary references are strewn throughout the book, and the story itself is set in a bookstore. In what way does the novel celebrate books? Give examples.

~ ~ ~

~ ~ ~

question 9

At the beginning of the book, the bookshop is barren and rarely patronized; but by the end, it becomes the mainstay of the island. How does the bookshop change the community's existence? Do you think it is a positive thing to have a bookshop in every community or not? Explain.

~ ~ ~

~ ~ ~

question 10

Daniel has multiple affairs, but he always returns to his wife and tells her he loves her. Do you believe in Daniel's love for his wife, Ismay? Give reasons for your answer.

~ ~ ~

~~~

question 11

Ismay stole the *Tamerlane* manuscript. What is your opinion of
the reason she gave for stealing it? Was it acceptable or not?
Explain your answer.

~~~

~ ~ ~

question 12

Maya won second place in a writing competition; thus, AJ begins to take her seriously as a writer. Do you believe that Maya has a future as an author, or is AJ just biased? Explain your answer.

~ ~ ~

~~~

question 13

AJ organized a book reading event to help promote his bookstore. What is the most interesting thing about the book reading event with Leon Friedman?

~~~

~ ~ ~

question 14

Maya is able to come to terms with her abandonment because she thinks that all children are left in stores, and she is the lucky one because she was left in a bookstore. How does Maya's reconciliation with the idea of being abandoned in a bookshop make you feel?

~ ~ ~

~ ~ ~

question 15

Maya was abandoned in AJs bookshop and after a few days, he decided to adopt her. Why do you think AJ wanted to adopt Maya? Do you think this was a good decision for both Maya and AJ? Give evidence from the book to support your answer.

~ ~ ~

~ ~ ~

question 16

The Washington Post reviewer, Keith Donohue has mentioned that the book is optimistic about the future of books and bookstores. Do you agree? What is your opinion about the future of bookstores and where we are heading from a literary viewpoint?

~ ~ ~

~ ~ ~

question 17

Pam Norfolk, a reviewer from *Blackpool Gazette,* says that *The Storied Life of AJ Fikry* is about books, but books are also about the people who read them. What do you infer from this statement?

~ ~ ~

~~~

question 18

The Storied Life of AJ Fikry made it to the top ten list of the *Library Journal*, a publication for librarians. Do you think it merits the honor? Why or why not?

~~~

~ ~ ~

question 19

The readers of *Goodreads* have given the book an average rating of nearly four stars. What would you rate it and why?

~ ~ ~

~~~

question 20

The Storied Life of AJ Fikry was originally published as *The Collected Works of A.J. Fikry.* How do you think this change in title has affected the reception of the book by readers?

~~~

~~~

question 21

Every cliché has been thrown into the mix in *The Storied Life of AJ Fikry*, or so claims Saima Hussain of *The Dawn*. What clichés did you notice in the book? Do you think they add any value to the story?

~~~

~ ~ ~

question 22

Hans Weyandt's review in the *Star Tribune* claims that Fikry and his friends are easy to cheer for. Do you agree? What is it about the characters that would make him say that?

~ ~ ~

~ ~ ~

question 23

The Storied Life of AJ Fikry made it to the fifteenth spot on the *New York Times* bestseller list. Why do you think this book was so well received by the reading community?

~ ~ ~

~ ~ ~

question 24

The Storied Life of AJ Fikry is centered around books. Do you think that the popularity of e-books will affect this book's charm? In what ways?

~ ~ ~

~ ~ ~

question 25

Robert Wiersema of *The Globe and Mail* compares the book to, "Life happens when you're busy." Why and how is this quote applicable to *The Storied Life of AJ Fikry*?

~ ~ ~

~ ~ ~

question 26

The author made the main character an Indian and brought up
the issue of race once or twice without concentrating too much
of it in the book. What do you think she was trying to say by this
mention of race and racism?

~ ~ ~

~ ~ ~

question 27

The author has a clear message regarding the role of books and bookshops in a community. How much do you agree/disagree with her?

~ ~ ~

~ ~ ~

question 28

We know that Zevin has written a screenplay for a movie called *Conversations with Other Women.* Do you think that *The Storied Life of AJ Fikry* would lend itself well to a movie? Give reasons for your response.

~ ~ ~

~~~

question 29

Zevin belongs to a mixed race family. In what ways do you think
that the challenges of coming from a mixed race background
affect her work?

~~~

~ ~ ~

question 30

Zevin is known for her Young Adult novels. Do you think she was able to transcend well from the genre to other genres in some of her works? Why or why not?

~ ~ ~

~ ~ ~

question 31

If you were Amelia or Maya, would you have forced AJ to have a surgery knowing that his chances were limited or would you have agreed to his more practical solution of saving the money for the future? Explain your answer.

~ ~ ~

~ ~ ~

question 32

We have seen that Daniel had many affairs and wasn't emotionally available in his marriage. Ultimately, Ismay gives him an ultimatum and asks for a divorce. If you were Ismay, how would you have dealt with Daniel?

~ ~ ~

~ ~ ~

question 33

Maya was left in AJs bookstore. After grumbling about it for a while, AJ finally grows fond of her and decides to adopt her. If you were AJ, would you have adopted Maya? Why or why not?

~ ~ ~

~ ~ ~

question 34

Marian was a single mother, unable to provide for her child, Maya. She ultimately commits suicide thinking that someone else would take care of Maya. If you were in Marian's position, would you have made the same decision? Why or why not?

~ ~ ~

~~~

question 35

AJ purchased an old copy of *Tamerlane* as retirement insurance. If you were AJ, how would you have reacted to the theft of *Tamerlane*?

~~~

~~~

question 36

Ismay decided to leave Daniel because of his behavior. Do you think he was surprised by this? If you were Daniel, how would you react to Ismay telling you she did not love you any longer?

~~~

~~~

question 37

Maya was abandoned by her mother, who then committed suicide because she didn't feel she could take good care of her daughter. If you were in Maya's shoes, how would you feel about your biological mother?

~~~

~~~

question 38

Marian had a child with Daniel, who was married to Ismay. When Marian goes to ask for help from him, his wife meets her. How would you have helped Marian if you were in Ismay's shoes? Would you have helped her at all?

~~~

Quiz Questions

"Ready to Announce the Winners?"

Tip: Create a leaderboard and track scores to see who gets the most correct answers. Winners required. Prizes optional.

quiz question 1

As a toddler, Maya thought that all children were left in _____ at some point in their lives.

~ ~ ~

~~~

quiz question 2

True or False: Lambiase was instrumental in starting a book club in AJ's bookshop.

~~~

~~~

quiz question 3

_____ was responsible for the theft of Tamerlane.

~~~

~ ~ ~

quiz question 4

True or False: Marian abandoned Maya because she was irresponsible.

~ ~ ~

~ ~ ~

quiz question 5

True or False: Ismay wanted a divorce from Daniel.

~ ~ ~

~ ~ ~

quiz question 6

_____ discovers who stole the manuscript of Tamerlane.

~ ~ ~

~ ~ ~

quiz question 7

Maya wrote a short story called _____.

~ ~ ~

~ ~ ~

quiz question 8

The Storied Life of AJ Fikry was Zevin's _____ book.

~ ~ ~

~ ~ ~

quiz question 9

True or False: Zevin comes from a mixed race family.

~ ~ ~

~ ~ ~

quiz question 10

True or False: Zevin was most scared of booksellers' opinion of the book.

~ ~ ~

~ ~ ~

quiz question 11

Zevin's first book was called _____.

~ ~ ~

~ ~ ~

quiz question 12

True or False: Zevin has written screenplays as well as novels.

~ ~ ~

Quiz Answers

1. shops
2. True
3. Ismay
4. False; Marian abandoned Maya because she felt that someone responsible would look after her in the bookshop after she was dead.
5. True
6. Lambiase
7. A Trip to the Beach
8. eighth
9. True
10. True
11. Elsewhere
12. True

Ways to Continue Your Reading

EVERY month, our team runs through a wide selection of books to pick the best titles for readers and reading groups, and promotes these titles to our thousands of readers – sometimes with free downloads, sale dates, and additional brochures.

Want to register yourself or a book group? It's free and takes 1-click.

Register here.

On the Next Page...

Please write us your reviews! Any length would be fine but we'd appreciate hearing you more! We'd be SO grateful.

Till next time,

BookHabits

"Loving Books is Actually a Habit"